BIRTH
OF A
BUSINESS

Life and Times of a Start-Up

CORY TSUHAKO

The birth of a business: *life and times of a start-up.*

Copyright © 2013 by Cory Tsuhako

This publication is designed to provide accurate and authoritative information in regard to the subject matter covered. It is sold with the understanding that neither the author nor the publisher is engaged in rendering legal, accounting, financial or other professional service. If legal advice or other expert assistance is required, the services of a competent professional person should be sought.

The author specifically disclaims any liability, loss, or risk, personal or otherwise, which is incurred as a consequence, directly or indirectly, of the use and application of any of the comments of this work. As each business situation is unique questions regarding the practice of law, accounting, finance, and Christian therapy each situation should be addressed to an appropriate professional.

All scripture quotations, unless otherwise indicated, are taken from the Holy Bible, New International Version ®, NIV ®. Copyright © 1973, 1978, 1984, 2011 by Biblica, Inc. ™ Used by permission of Zondervan. All rights reserved worldwide. www.zondervan.com The "NIV" and "New International Version" are trademarks registered in the United States Patent and Trademark Office by Biblica, Inc™

People's names and certain details of their stories have been changed to protect the privacy of the individuals involved.

ISBN-13:978-1492122142
ISBN-10:1492122149

Categories

1.Business and Economics-Entrepreneurship. 2. Small business

Tsuhako, Cory 1962-

FIRST EDITION Published by Cory Tsuhako
Fonts used Palatino Linotype and Garamond

Book cover images from Shutterstock.com

Contents

"Where two or three meet in my Name, I am among them" (Matthew 18:19).

INTRODUCTION

At 9:00 a.m. Monday morning, you arrive at your office, turn on the computer, and make yourself a cup of coffee.

The sun is shining through your office window. As you gaze outside, the view looks brighter, more inviting than usual. You are free. No more "boss" looking over your shoulder. No one holding you back from reaching your destiny.

On the morning of your first day your adrenaline is running high. You lean back in your executive chair. Today is the first day of your new life, but where do you begin?

In the beginning it will surprise you that you're on your own...you are isolated. There are no clients, customers, or co-workers. You operate a business that won't be breaking even for five years. No one is keeping track of how many hours you'll work today.

Working part time helps, but to succeed, you have to work a lot of hours. This can go on for years. You notice the clicks of the clock echoing off the empty walls...tick, tick, tick.

CHAPTER ONE

Have you ever **dreamed of owning a business?** Does the lifestyle beckon you? Do you think you could do it? Think about it…would *you* want to work for you?

It's my goal, for you, the reader, to learn from my experiences of starting a business after business school. In this journey I hope to show you:

- Your Business Plan gets outdated quickly.
- A Business Plan helps you to Focus.
- You have to Focus for a short time.
- You may have to do SALES.
- It's hard to find people you can trust.
- In a start-up you might be the one taking out the trash.
- Starting your business will cost more than you think.
- Carefully select your business.

This Won't Be Easy…

If it was easy, then everyone would do it. Entrepreneurship isn't for everybody. If the uncertainty of knowing where your next paycheck will come from or if you have dependents to support you'll face:

- Risk
- Stress
- Uncertainty

It is my prayer that you can take something from this book to make the journey a little lighter.

The reality is...it's not easy

You may find comfort and encouragement reading books on Ben Franklin, Warren Buffett, and Richard Branson. Study the successful ones that came before you.

L et me first say that I've never taken a class on entrepreneurship. I thought I would learn it by osmosis, the way we learned the metric system. Students didn't take courses on the metric system; they just learned it by being in a science class. Unfortunately, business isn't that way. I thought that earning an MBA would teach me the skills I needed; it didn't. So I started a dental lab, made mistakes, and ran the business for 10 years.

Experience

I had no experience starting a business—studied business in college, and had experience in the dental industry, *but no experience starting a business.* Starting a business was more challenging than I expected! I thought I knew everything necessary. I didn't know what I didn't know.

Experience Counts...I had *no experience* in starting a business and neither did my partner. It's important to involve proven, experienced people at the outset of your business. We had investors who believed in us-who had confidence we could deliver a successful business.

When you are the one with the least experience of the group it may be time to swallow your pride and learn basic business principles. This is the school of hard knocks; trying, failing, learning, applying lessons, trying again. It's something like a baby learning how to walk.

How can someone gain experience starting a business?

See One, Do One, and Teach One.

Go ahead and open a business for the experience. It's certainly a great learning experience as you will progress in developing new skills. A typical business has a life-cycle of ten years, but only 50 percent of new businesses survive past five years.

I wish I had started several businesses before this one. It would have been better to have some experience. This data would have been valuable. If you have a passion for something, you may even consider starting a business to gain experience.

This is your training time. This is similar to a baby learning to crawl, walk, and then run. In your developmental years you are learning to crawl. Eventually you get the confidence and enough scraped knees to begin to run. In this entrepreneurial life, you are expected to run a 5K right away.

B-School

In my opinion, an entrepreneur doesn't need an MBA to be successful. What's more important is previous experience in starting and running a business, a strong work ethic, experience in your industry, ability to delegate to professionals (CPA, lawyers, and Consultants), the ability to lead and train, the ability to focus on one thing at a time, and the flexibility and wisdom to find your niche. Another important thing is to manage your sales force and to keep your marketing department running.

It's important to get good mentors who will teach you. A good team will expand your skills, help with decision making, expand networks, help in marketing and raising money, sharing in technology, and will make the experience easier.

A good team will:

- Increase your skills
- Help with decision making
- Expand your networking
- Assist in marketing
- Raise capital
- Share in technology

The MBA degree trains **managers** of business. The MBA has the ability to manage, sell, promote, and utilize business functions valuable in a business. They have to deal with what is happening today and progress towards future goals like everyone else.

But I'm an MBA...

Only you care about this. Some companies may be impressed by your credentials and may offer you special discounts, but you still have to prove you are worthy of their trust.

Sometimes an MBA can hurt your chances of success. After completing my MBA I thought it was the end of school. It was the beginning. When starting a business there's much to learn from locating suppliers, finding customers, networking, accounting and invoicing software, to being self-disciplined.

Are you confident because you have a master's degree? Not in the entrepreneur world. This is another world. This is the first day of school.

You may be alone

As you progress, you may realize that business school didn't prepare you for this. While in school, you felt you could take on any business and turn it into a success.

This isn't easy

What you learned in business school did not prepare you for entrepreneurship. It's hard work. There's a steep learning curve. You will do labor. A lot of time should be spent on sales. This will be a real-world Ph.D. There will be mistakes. You'll learn things about yourself you didn't know.

You may lose friends along the journey. Make failures small and manageable and learn to analyze them.

Having MBA classmates can hurt your chances of success. Imagine this. You will spend time debating which accounting software to use. People want to work with software they know. Some may question your commitment and will impose their goals on the business. They will shout, panic, and insult you. The MBA degree is known for BIG money, and most start-ups are small. We had three MBAs in a small business commonly started by a trade person. No one wanted to water plants or throw out the trash.

Where did I go wrong? A case study feels differently when you are reading about it, than when you are living it. In the real world:

- Employees don't show up
- Act unprofessional
- Don't do their responsibilities

Starting Your Own Business is Not Like Business School

Guess who throws out the trash? It might be you. Do you want to pay someone to do things you can do yourself? It's probably not a good idea to pay someone for things you can do yourself.

In school the answers are in the books. Every question has an answer. In this business you will manage disrespectful employees who question your knowledge and experience, and you may run out of money.

It's difficult

Complement your MBA (or anyone for that matter) with these skills.

>**S**-ales

>**A**-ccounting

>**L**-eadership

>**E**-ntrepreneurship

Concentrate on "S.A.L.E." activities to keep your skills growing and developing. Having a reputation for quality will make it easier to set higher prices.

You never know when the next sale may occur

How an MBA helps...

- Credibility
- Education & Training
- Financial Management
- Marketing
- Networking opportunities
- Strategy

B-Plan

"Plans fail for lack of counsel, but with many advisors they succeed" (Proverbs 15:22).

The Business Plan

I was so confident the business plan would work. I was confused why my partners didn't want to read it. The "plan" was granted an honors grade and was in the school library. Reading it ten years later shows how inaccurate it can be. The business plan should be revised at least one time a year.

If anything can be learned from this exercise it would be to be focused. But don't let it limit you from working with others that your business plan didn't cover. Sometimes a client or competitor will create an opportunity that you didn't consider.

Don't go chasing opportunities. It's very difficult to be both focused and flexible at the same time. That's why you will hear people say regarding business, "It's not easy." It's not.

In my case the business strayed from the plan. It wasn't much help except on occasions it limited the business to focus on something that wasn't working well. It was hard to imagine the finished product while in the present moment.

- Focus on the present business.
- If you must start a new business, do it with the profits from the first business.

Can you afford a mistake?

What works today...

May not work tomorrow. Things change quickly with technology, regulations, laws, taxes, and competition. Be prepared to be flexible if things are not going your way. Look for opportunities that have good economics, ability to raise prices with inflation, a growing industry, no robotics, no trend towards outsourcing overseas and consolidation. If your industry is experiencing rapidly changing technology, complacency may put you out of business.

But My Business Plan is Fantastic!

It may be good for a few weeks to a month if lucky. Generally it restricts when you need to be researching, testing, and experimenting. It keeps you focused but can hold you back from testing and trying things. It has a tendency to confine you. Reality check...no one cares about your business plan...except you.

Execute Your Plan?

You must build a great team. Everything has to progress at the same time to get ahead. It's impossible to move an entire business according to the business plan by yourself. You have to raise capital and some mistakes will be made. A common mistake is to start too many businesses before one is profitable. But if the main business isn't working you need plan B to survive.

What, five years to break even?

"Be of sober spirit, be on the alert...And after you have suffered for a little while, the God of all grace...will Himself perfect, confirm, strengthen and establish you" (1 Peter 5:8-10).

When it was told to me (by my professors) that it takes five years to break even, I thought to myself, "That's you, not me. I have the team, the education, and more experience." It's amazing how long it takes to break even. Equipment breaks, supplies need to be ordered, taxes (be prepared to pay four times a year if a sole proprietorship) have to be paid, technology needs to be upgraded, and people need to be paid.

There's a reason why they say it. As you grow your business you need to hire more people, which increases your costs. Leading up to the fifth year things tend to break, investors grow impatient, you overspend on marketing.

If you grow a new area of the business, supplies and equipment need to be purchased. Something always seems to come up. Some businesses may even take longer! Do you have the time, money, and support to keep going?

At first, several competitors asked me to help with their marketing. I gave them the same answer, "Oh, we don't help our competitors." My thinking was if it was not in the business plan then we shouldn't do it. We needed to be focused, right? After awhile I realized that the business plan offered little in direction.

TEAM

"Two are better than one, because they have a good return for their work: If one falls down, his friend can help him up. But pity the man who falls and has no one to help him up"
(Ecclesiastes 3:9-12).

A Good Partner is someone who complements your skills; shares your passions; is honest, hard-working, disciplined; a good listener; likes to have fun; easy to be around; and respectful. If you form a team, your team can make up for your shortcomings.

- Brings different skills
- Shares your goals
- Honest
- Hard-working
- Disciplined
- Easy to get along with
- Fun

We all know that a good team wins. A good team will always beat a *genius individual* in intelligence tests. But how do you find a partner you can trust?

For me it was not a good idea to pick a business school classmate. Sometimes our classmates are our peers. If they are our competitors it's hard for them to help us to succeed. Take your time. Be patient in picking your partners. It's like rushing into a marriage. You probably wouldn't do it. Use a trial period like dating. It's crucial to pick wisely. Look at great sports teams, great partnerships, successful marriages, families, and other successful organizations. You may want to pick professionals so you can see what kind of talent is available. This way if you make a mistake you can just go on to another CPA or lawyer. Can you get a retired business owner? Sometimes they are looking for things to do.

"Where two or three meet in my Name, I am among them"
(Matthew 18:19).

Take your time. Don't rush this important decision. Time has a way of working things out.

My biggest mistake was selecting a VC (venture capitalist or banker) as a partner, another classmate who is an operations manager, a relative who was more an investor than a working partner, an investor, and an experienced dental technician who was my friend in school whose goal in life wasn't to work for me.

Let's say that you and I are partners. If we assume that it's going to take approximately five years to break even, we are probably going to be losing money each month, for

16

years. This is our core business and what we do best. If we try a side business and it doesn't work out we may have used the capital we needed just to survive up to the fifth year. It makes sense to pick a partner who lives below his means.

"A man's wisdom gives him patience" (Proverbs 19:11).

Partners...a long time ago I had a partner. Let me introduce you to her. She was as loyal as can be. Her name was Primsy, a German shepherd and Husky mix. When I left for school she waited for my return. When looking for a partner, the entrepreneur should look for a partner as loyal as their dog.

Can you trust your partner as much as your dog?

If not, can you keep looking?

A business partnership is like a marriage.

"Though one may be overpowered, two can defend themselves. A cord of three strands is not quickly broken." (Ecclesiastes 3:12).

Venture Capitalists or better known as "Vulture Capitalists"

No, don't do it. It's tempting. They seem like they have access to money. Sometimes they are salespeople. They sell loans for a living. They are not miracle workers you are better off without them. If friendships and good relations are important to you, then just say no and form a stronger team. They are not your friends nor do they want to be. In my case what I needed was an experienced dental lab partner, somebody who would complement my skills. What I got was a VC waiting for the right time to sell his equity and didn't want to get his hands dirty. He increased the level of mistrust at the outset. You may not know the person they sell their interest to.

If they had so much money why would they want part of yours? To sell their shares for a profit so they can own their own business.

Parents

There's a very important distinction between a parent who wants to help their child in their business and a working partner. A parent who invests money and helps out whenever they can is an investor and or a silent partner. A working partner with equity in the business is someone who will be working as hard as you, shoulder to shoulder, day after day for hopefully 10 years. Don't make the costly mistake of making a parent a working partner with equity. The people in your team will leave.

Find Partner Companies

That will benefit from your success. Sometimes, they will act as your strategic partners. A dependable delivery company can be very important to your success. A temporary administrative assistant can be a strong ally for you as well as a marketing agency. If you can surround yourself with these stakeholders, they can work as your ideal partners without giving up equity.

Skilled laborers are another thing…

- They are difficult to manage.
- They will disrespect you in some form or another.
- They are hard to replace…and difficult to manage.
- They will want more money.
- In time they will drive you crazy.

Some options are to:

- Outsource your skilled labor.
- Outsource some administrative & marketing duties.
- Become cross-trained.
- Become a specialist.

TEAM…your key to a successful life:

A good lawyer and CPA are necessary to your business success. Having a good coach, advisor, and consultant can do wonders for your team. A team to keep your family running smoothly can be useful, giving you more time to spend with them or working longer hours. Consider hiring a courier service to make those long trips for you. Entrepreneurship is a daily grind if you are the oldest child. Can you delegate the day-to-day managing of the business to a middle child? How about a youngest child to help with sales? They are great at social things like throwing parties.

Know what you are good at, or, know thyself

Some people are better at starting things (the oldest child). Others are more flexible and can deal with people better (middle), while others like to deal with people (youngest).

Which one are you?

- ❏ Starting a business-Oldest child
- ❏ Day-to-day management-Middle child (best entrepreneurs).
- ❏ Sales-Youngest child

Which one are you? Are you spending time on your strengths?

This stuff is hard

This stuff is hard. If it was easy then everyone would be self-employed. Watch your health and get plenty of rest and exercise. Innovation thinking time: you will need those walks in the park to clear your mind.

Find a partner who thinks differently.

Don't Try to Manage the Unmanageable.

The undisciplined people in the business will challenge and frustrate you. Trust them to carry out important duties and you will spend your time worrying if things will get done.

Your "partner" shows up to the business after a couple of weeks of not showing up because you ask why they aren't coming by.

Dialogue:

Undisciplined person: "Hi, what can I do to help?"

You, the owner of the business: "Can you make a delivery to this client?"

Undisciplined person: "Sure."

After cleaning and/or answering the phone (while reading the paper), you wonder if they will be going.

Undisciplined person: "Well, I guess I'm too tired to make that delivery, now that I've been here."

You, the owner: "You mean I have to make that delivery myself now?"

Undisciplined person: "Can you? I'm too tired."

You, the owner: "I guess. I wasn't planning on it after you said you would go." You get ready to deliver and decide whether to come back to the office.

You get upset, you don't see your partner for about a month and the cycle continues.

This is so disruptive. It would have been better to call the courier in the first place. This is not a working partner. It's more like having a volunteer.

Know the difference between a well meaning investor/volunteer and a working partner.

What would you do?

Picking the wrong people at the early stage of your business can ruin the best of businesses. You should remove the wrong people out of the business in order to succeed. It's not easy, but business isn't easy.

What happens to the 50% of businesses that fail to make it to year five?

- ☹ Bad credit
- ☹ Burn out
- ☹ Loss of friends
- ☹ Tarnished reputation

Would You Take This Deal?

During our first year we ran out of capital. A classmate made an interesting offer. Robert was an international student who wanted to stay in the U.S. so he offered 100K for 51% of the business. He would stay out of the day-to-day decisions but wanted input on four major decisions. It was noted that this industry wasn't good, but we could make profits. Then the profits would then be invested elsewhere. Robert had a master's in business and was working on his second. His family was wealthy and his wife was a CPA.

At this point I had spent a lot of time on equity matters (who owned what percent of the business). He wanted to buy my partner's shares.

Me: 51%

Jack: 30%

Relative: 14%

Gerry: 5%

At this point in the business my partners were no longer present. They didn't come by anymore. Pick the wrong team and you will suffer in the future. I was working as a one-person dental lab.

What happened?

I declined the offer despite opposition from classmates (I started this business while attending business school). They thought he possessed the capital and skills that my current partners didn't offer. In time he started a business, found a job, had a special needs child, and returned to his country. If I had accepted his offer it probably wouldn't have turned out well.

If a business has robotics and outsourcing overseas, then it is not a good industry. The use of robotics increases the investment in operations. Outsourcing overseas makes for cheaper prices which makes it harder to raise prices.

It's important to learn everything you can before opening your business. This way you can focus on growing the business, and managing your marketing.

For me, it was difficult to learn with so many distractions. If felt like my time wasn't my own. At other times you may be too tired. It's important to create a learning company.

Note: Do your due diligence, as you may be responsible for your partner's debts in certain types of business structures.

Talk to your lawyer about which business structure suits you the best.

Trust

"Trust in the Lord with all your heart and lean not on your own understanding; in all your ways acknowledge him, and he will make your paths straight" (Proverbs 3:5-6).

Who Can You Trust? Can you even trust yourself?

Family

Best advice? Make time for them. Appreciate them and respect their importance in your life. It's best that you appreciate them, as you may not see them as much. You don't want that to become a problem.

Don't rely on family and friends to build your future empire. It is not their dream to work for you. Build your business on the right people and save yourself the heartache. In my experience it applied to classmates as well. How can parents help their children without conflict?

- Buy them a helpful book
- Magazine subscription
- Don't socialize with workers unless absolutely necessary-this is their place of work and their company.
- Avoid creating a dysfunctional situation
- Pick up children from school

- Offer to do food shopping
- Help around the house: cooking, watering yard and plants
- Cleaning yard and house
- Cooking and sharing food
- Don't call office
- Stay away from office if possible
- Don't pit siblings against one another

Basically, it's your children's business. Try to stay away from the business. You can support them in their personal life. A parent at work can result in a dysfunctional environment that isn't good for leading. Ask yourself how many times did your parents visit you at work and socialize with your co-workers?

Be Careful of Your Family

During my first year of the business, I was left to care for my grandmother who had Alzheimer's. You won't be able to juggle your time to oversee someone who is so dependent. People around you may not realize how busy you are. Think long and hard before watching a child or sick grandparent. People around you must understand the time pressures you have. You can only do one thing well.

Starting and running your own business is very demanding. You should work somewhere between 60-80 hours per week. At 10-12 hours per day, plus sleep, it leaves little time for a social life, family life, networking with clients, continuing education (because without learning you will not grow), spiritual life, exercise, quiet time to reflect, friends, developing new relationships, and reading. There's marketing, sales, accounting, phones, taking out the trash, cleaning. What about your relationships? Are there demands on your time? What about hobbies? You may want to do a time management analysis and see where you are spending your minutes.

Clients and Customers...

May take up most of your time. Without them, you are out of business, so it's a top priority to be available 8-10 hours of your day. You should reserve time for reading, family, exercise, and fun.

You will find people who want to do business with you. If you are open, honest, and trustworthy you can develop a mutual trust for one another. Treat them well and repay them with your loyalty. It's true what they say "the more you help others, the more they will help you."

Mentors...

Mentors are important. They can make or break you, except it's hard to distinguish who is really behind you. If they have learned on their own, they may have some valuable insights that can be useful to you.

"You should double your price." If it was that easy I would. This was advice given to me. If I followed that advice, we would have surely lost our clients. Know why your clients do business with you before making drastic decisions. Give yourself a week. Know that every action has a reaction.

How can you find people you can trust to stay with the company long term? It's very hard to find a partner who will stay committed long term. Some will find a job; others may lose interest. Put it in writing and agree on an exit plan.

FAITH

"Therefore...be steadfast, immovable...your toil is not in vain in the Lord" (1 Corinthians 15:58).

Entrepreneurship is so hard I can't imagine doing it without God's help.

It's that challenging...

I am a Christian. Faith is the top priority in my life and I wished I had been more disciplined during these last 10 years of business. It was difficult to attend church when I was so busy, but I did sense God's calling.

It will be good to have a higher power who will comfort you. You won't have as much free time as before, and there will be demands on your time.

"I can do all things through Christ who strengthens me."
(Philippians 4:13)

With all the challenges and demands that will be put on you, it is important to be able to pray and leave your concerns at God's feet. He will give you a peace and will give you stability in a life that is so unpredictable.

I wasn't involved in church at this time, but some people may get strength from serving others. Don't forget that your plate is full and you will have enough to do throughout the week. Adding meetings, rehearsing, fellowship, attending Sunday worship services, and mid-week Bible studies might make you too busy. Follow your heart; you will know if God is calling you to serve. You are representing Christ to the people who you meet, as this is your mission field. Churches have Christian business meetings and this could be a good meeting. If not, consider creating your own support group.

If you have selected a good team then there's no reason your spiritual life should suffer. The Bible tells us to go to church and worship with fellow believers. We need this support to grow in our walk with Christ.

"Lazy hands make a man poor, but diligent hands bring wealth"
(Proverbs 10:4).

If you are too busy to go to church, you can make time by listening to messages on TV, Internet, and radio. There is a wealth of messages on YouTube and the large churches have their messages streaming online. Reading the Bible, listening to worship music while you work, quiet time, and prayer help to keep you connected to God's family.

In my opinion a support fellowship group of four to seven people can help. Members of the group can give and receive support, read books, discuss DVDs and videos, be coached as a group, listen to speakers, share prayer requests and concerns. Peer-to-peer coaching and fellowship can help in keeping you grounded in your faith.

"As the body without the spirit is dead, so faith without deeds is dead." (James 2:26).

How to make your own Church service (if too busy)

"If you keep your feet from breaking the Sabbath and from doing as you please on my holy day, if you call the Sabbath a delight and the Lord's day honorable, and if you honor it by not going your own way and not doing as you please or speaking idle words, then you will find your joy in the LORD, and I will cause you to ride on the heights of the land and to feast on the inheritance of your father Jacob." (Isaiah 58: 13-14).

It's always best to attend a worship service with fellow believers. But certain times you are too busy to attend. In these cases:

- ✞ Prayer and quiet time
- ✞ Message
- ✞ Bible reading
- ✞ Memory verse
- ✞ Worship music
- ✞ Spend time developing your talent
- ✞ Tithe
- ✞ Fellowship
- ✞ Ministry

✝ Watch a short leadership video

Seven spiritual things that can get your business and self on track:

1. Commit to reading the entire Bible.
2. Honor Sundays by either attending church or making a church-like schedule if you are too busy.
3. Devotions first thing upon waking up.
4. Quiet time and prayer.
5. Dedicate each day to God.
6. Ask him to use you today.
7. Tell him that you are available.

"Do not wear yourself out to get rich: have the wisdom to show restraint" (Proverbs 23:4).

Vision and Goals

"Let your light shine before men is such as way that they may see your good works, and glorify your Father who is in heaven" (Matthew 5:16).

Why does your business exist?

Who do you serve?

Advice?

It may be a good idea (if your business allows it) to start from home at the beginning. You can have a snack, watch TV, check on stocks, do housework, run a load of clothes, water the yard, and play with your dog, all while waiting on responses to your marketing. If you over estimated the demand for your products and services, at least you don't have a long-term lease.

For seven months we had an office with no sales-think about that. We paid rent on the space, had a lease on equipment, as well as licenses and taxes, bank fees, car insurance, DSL, and phones.

I suggest you wait on the office. Create a legacy of making do with less. It's sound financial management people will understand. Wait, wait, and wait on the office!

MARKETING

Who knows your business, and your products, better than you do? Initially, you may be THE BEST salesperson in your company.

Marketing Materials

Everything is communicating your company, from direct mail, brochures, flyers, website, blogs, social media, and sales.

Are you a person people trust? Don't let others discourage you from sales; it's where everything is taking place.

If Your Partner Isn't a Marketing Expert ...

It's important to keep you motivated. Some books I found entertaining are Seth Godin's *Purple Cow*, and Paul Arden's *It's Not How Good You Are It's How Good You Want To Be*. Ad Age is a nice website. *Sales and Marketing Management* magazine is another good source of information.

We tried several people to manage our marketing department. No one has the depth of knowledge except you, the owner. Who knows you better than yourself? You have the passion to speak the language of business with other owners. People who have started a business prefer to help fellow entrepreneurs more than they would a salesperson.

"Jabez cried out to the God of Israel, Oh, that you would bless me and enlarge my territory! Let your hand be with me, and keep me from harm so that I will be free from pain. And God granted his request" (1 Chronicles 4:10).

Metrics

Tracking your marketing efforts can lead to increased sales-it's true what they say about what you track gets done. Ignore your marketing department and your sales will decline. It's important to stay on top of this.

Marketing Metrics

Type of Marketing	M	T	W	TH	F
Direct Mail					
Magazine ad					
Online					
Social Media					
Sales					
Totals					

You can make a list that matches your company but you should give each a weight of importance. For example, a direct mailing might get one point where a lunch with a prospective client may get fifteen points. A marketing metric of at least 100 per week with a cash bonus for a score of 500 may get the job done. You know what the business needs better than anyone.

That which you track gets done

Marketing Planning

Marketing: Jan Feb March April May June July Aug

Website   ---

Magazine   ---------------------------------------

Video   ------------------------------------

Your marketing efforts are proportional to sales. The more time spent on promotions the higher revenue. Just be sure that you are making profits, not losing money per sale.

Nothing happens without a sale

Try this Exercise...

Go to a quiet room. Close the door, turn on your computer, and sit in silence. For the first few months, you will be working alone waiting on responses from your marketing efforts. This may take six months or more. Sometimes, it's hard to break through the noise. The sayings were right. Marketing efforts take about six months. I hope you will have planned well and will hit the ground running with clients already. Phone calls will be coming through; people will be visiting you, there will be people to hire and train, meetings with investors, and clients to meet.

Journal entry from year one: "My partner said I reminded him of Tom Hanks from the movie, *Cast Away*. I'm in the office alone, with just a goldfish, a few plants, a radio, and computer to keep me company. There's no work to create in terms of manufacturing a product; everything is related to getting clients." After months of this, I started to venture into the nice weather we have in sunny California. So I turned on call forwarding and went to the beach, took golf lessons, and played golf and tennis.

During these times guess who would call before I was about to make my 10 foot putt? Yes, you guessed right a client asking me information about the business, if I could send information to them. They would realize I was either walking on the pier or on a golf course. Naturally, this didn't go over too well. So it was back to the office. I went back to marketing machine mode but went out to lunch. Guess who would be calling on their lunch breaks? It seems like clients and customers prefer to call on their lunch breaks!

In time, things got busier, people came and went, and the business progressed. But…things were slow at the start. I should have spent more time:

- Building relationships with future clients
- Learning everything I needed on sales
- Gaining specialized knowledge and abilities on the product
- Visiting with past employers
- Networking with competitors
- Streamlining our marketing department

This should have been done before quitting my job and renting an office.

You are a Salesperson...What?!

It's not easy being in the salesperson role. In my 10 years in business, I talked with owners, and they told me things like this.

"This is sales, not Marketing!"

"This business owns me, I don't own it."

"This is not like the books..."

"I don't like sales..."

I didn't like sales, although I did it. Someone in your company will sell or you won't be in business. Clients will want you to educate them on the latest developments in your particular industry and on new products. You speak the language of business. It seemed more a sharing of information. Make their problems important to you and you can be a trusted colleague.

It helps to send them a referral or two when they need customers, clients, and workers. Helping them with their business concerns is another way you can increase your value.

I observed times where entrepreneurs have gone door-to-door selling puppies for a dog grooming shop; another entrepreneur went door-to-door selling his car insurance. I tried visiting dental offices and can say that it was not fun. By doing this, you'll see firsthand why your marketing efforts are either succeeding or failing.

More Sales...

You will find that nothing happens without a sale. Look around...who is most qualified? Hate to say this, but it's you, the owner/entrepreneur. You speak the customer's language and live your story. You are best qualified to sell your vision, purpose, the products and services. A salesperson can't sell you like you can. Get out there and sell. You will realize that without sales you can't pay the bills.

How do you become a great salesperson? It helps to talk with effective sales reps. They often will share what they know, as most clients don't ask questions like, "Why are you so great at sales?"

Books and videos on sales can also help. YouTube has many videos on sales greats from Zig Ziglar to Grant Cardone.

Sales is something between teaching, acting, and communicating. It's similar to entertaining. You have to entertain potential customers when you have their attention, then present information in a way that will make them curious, and help them solve problems.

Trust is important and you must be honest if you want them to keep coming back. Always be HONEST!

There are push and pull elements to sales. It helps to have a special discount/offer on their first purchase to reduce their risk. Offer a percentage discount on the first order; give them a free item to close the sale. Follow-up may be necessary to land a sale, and a thank you card is a nice way to start a new business relationship. You are putting in the effort to show them that they are important to your business.

Don't take yourself so seriously...

Learn to laugh. It's a steep learning curve to think that you have to be a salesperson. It's not fun, but may be necessary to get sales and cash flow into the company. In my opinion, it's better to get an office after the initial sales results. Sometimes it may take six months or more to get a first sale, and a feeling of desperation may happen if the rent is due. It may depend upon what kind of business you are in. If you can outsource labor and bring the product in-house this may work better. Also, you may have opportunities to help competitors and clients in marketing other services. In time, you may be able to move your marketing department "out of house." Your business can be its major client, handle a few outside clients and your marketing department can be a stand-alone business. Add consulting from the knowledge that you are gaining everyday and a consulting/marketing agency may be possible.

You will make mistakes. It's okay. It's how you learn... but it's these mistakes that can put you out of business.

Takes a lot of commitment

Make it fun

Come up with ideas to make your marketing efforts fun! Try giveaways, contests, free stuff, donuts to keep you and your customers interested.

Best Practices

You are the sales rep in your company. You are also the spokesperson. Is your company producing an excellent product? How many steps would it take to make it a world's best product or service? Compare the investment with other options. Manage your growth slowly...at the beginning of your business you are going to lose money.

Delegation...

Try to delegate little by little. You need a group of talented individuals to win. At first it's difficult to even delegate dropping off marketing materials at the post office. You may wonder if it was thrown in the trash. Managing your marketing department is crucial in the event of an important client leaving, getting sick, retiring, or dying. When busy, marketing is easy to put off.

FINANCIAL MANAGEMENT

"Honor the Lord with your wealth, with the first fruits of all your crops; then your barns will be filled to overflowing, and your vats will brim over with new wine" (Proverbs 3:9-10).

Accounting anyone?

I hope you enjoy accounting and bookkeeping. I didn't and guess what I was doing every day? Preparing invoices, bookkeeping, taxes, checking my bank account, collecting money, recording accounts receivables and paying bills.

It's best to know the accounting systems **before** the first day of business. You'll be better off focusing your time on getting clients instead of learning new accounting and billing software. Do the work before you open. Hit the ground running!

After you get clients be sure to dig into the invoices to analyze your data. You can use the data to predict busy months, when your clients are most likely to take vacations, industry and company trends, and the best times to increase your marketing and advertising efforts.

Use data to predict:

- Busiest times of the year

- Vacations

- Industry trends

- Company sales trends

- Best time to start marketing

You may want to hire a CPA/bookkeeper who can help you understand what your numbers and trends mean. However, CPAs prefer to serve businesses that are making substantial profits. You may want to consider using a student.

Know how much profit you are making and be sure you can cover your expenses. Have at least six months of cash available just in case your clients change to your competition.

- Keep technology costs as low as possible
- Embrace a frugal lifestyle
- Surround yourself with positive people
- Charge enough for your product
- Rarely use your credit card
- What you can do, do yourself
- New and innovative is risky
- Don't over commit on purchases
- Find creative ways to reduce risk

Taxes

...are a headache and they come up **four** times a year. If you do taxes yourself, you will find yourself doing your company's taxes and your personal income tax. This will make you busy.

*Note: Your taxes most likely will be due in January, April, July, and October. What is due is the state sales tax you collect from your sales plus a district tax (this is in California). Any questions and the Board of Equalization can refer you to classes they offer. Pre-save for January...this month has the most expense including the City license, quarterly tax, Christmas gifts and special end of year prices.

Taxes, continued ...

You are charged a yearly assessment tax of 1% of all business assets. On large pieces of equipment (roughly $10K), there is a separate assessment tax on that asset. As the asset depreciates let them know and they will adjust the value of the asset (your payment).

Financial Management

It's not a good idea to compete on price. If you're the low price leader, there will always be a new business to under price you. If the reason your clients/customers are working with you is that you are the lowest price they may leave when there is someone cheaper.

- Sell things you don't need (inventory)
- Buy and invest in things that will go up in value
- Raise prices a little every year

Profit and loss statement

What is a profit and loss statement? I didn't know what this was so here it is. Example: You have a business that is making $1,000 in revenue per month with expenses of $500 per month.

Revenue – Expenses = Profit or (loss)

Example:

Revenues of $1,000

Expenses $500

$1,000 - $500 = $500 profit

The profit and loss statement seemed to be the best snapshot of how the business was doing on a daily basis combined with an online checking account.

A ratio that is helpful is the profit margin per unit sold. Or, how much money you are making per sale, per square footage or per inventory turnover.

Become familiar with your financial tools that you need: balance sheet, profit and loss statement and income statement.

Investing: I started day trading at my last job. We doubled the company brokerage account and the owner's IRAs in four months. When the tech bubble burst, I sold, they held and bought more technology stocks as the market went down and an account that once was $8K turned to $300.

Get the company brokerage account set up before you start your business. Setting up accounts and dealing with banks can be a distraction from growing and managing the business.

I would recommend the study of Warren Buffett to any entrepreneur, new or experienced. The lessons on frugality, value investing and business in general are worth their weight in gold.

After reading *Security Analysis* by Benjamin Graham and *The Intelligent Investor* by Benjamin Graham and David Dodd, I changed my investment style to a value investing approach.

Make a habit of buying things that go up in value, not down. Buying shares of the best growth stock when it's on sale may be better than buying a piece of equipment. One day it will break and will have a resale value of zero. In 1982 my dream car cost $5,000 and later sold for $125; Berkshire Hathaway stock has gone from $19 to $160,000.

Investment A vs. Investment B

Before investing the time and money to pursue an opportunity, you may want to do a comparative analysis to see which investment stacks up better than the other. For example, an investment in Google versus getting that equipment you've been wanting to buy.

Avoid that large investment in innovative equipment. What happens in five years? It breaks and newer equipment comes out. In time the resale value will be $0. Then the equipment needs to be replaced.

An investment in Microsoft, Google, Berkshire:

- Goes up in price
- Doesn't require labor
- Appreciates
- Passive income

Become a student of Warren Buffett. I read most of his books and learned something from each one.

Can you bootstrap your business?

Nothing is more wasteful than having an office that you are not using. An office rent is one of the largest expense items. Postponing the office rent makes good sense. When the rent becomes due with no revenue it puts the entrepreneur on a roller coaster of emotions. Do you absolutely need the office space? Sometimes it helps to have office space after getting some customers.

In my opinion, the entrepreneur should start small and grow slowly. Then grow businesses around your main business.

Can you earn some consulting money? Marketing services can also help pay the rent. A part-time job could help during those slow months. At this time, you should be open minded and willing to see what opportunities come your way. Don't turn down opportunities to work with competitors and past employers.

If you will be losing a little money on each sale, it's important to keep your steady paychecks with a part-time job, providing consulting or services. At the beginning of your venture, the challenge will be to make a profit after paying expenses.

Sometimes your competition may be looking for people to collaborate with. Let people know what you are looking for and you may be surprised who may help you. For example, I was interested in sharing an office so I asked a salesperson. He asked around and found someone who was looking to sublease some office space. He was located just five miles away.

Don't refuse working with someone because it's not in your business plan. Be open minded, as you never know where your next business opportunity will come from. The business plan dilemma is that it will keep you too focused when you need to be flexible to find your niche. In time, you will need to focus on the business at hand before going after every opportunity.

What helps, what doesn't?

Getting a space. First, you should do a lot of research on the location. Find a place that is safe, with easy access, but not where there is too much traffic (for a service business … a retail business is different). A location close to home is a luxury that you won't regret with nice parking, low crime and a nice landlord. Starting from home is my best recommendation if you can do it this way.

Frugal, frugal, frugal

A penny saved is a penny earned. Use your time wisely to stretch your dollars. Growing a garden can be a better hobby than watching the news. A vegan diet is a great way to save money, as you can grow your own food. Make it a challenge. It's good for your health, your pocketbook, and your business.

It's easier to save a buck than to make one

99-cent store
This store is great. Office supplies can be purchased for $1.00. Food, drinks, batteries, plants, cards, towels, clothes, cleaning supplies can all be picked up for a dollar.

More money saving ideas

Comparison shop. Look at it as a challenge to find the best deals. The best deal on computer paper was at a major supermarket. Be a chef and eat in.

Use your library card!
Almost any book you need is at the public or university library. It is good to get out of the box.

If you must purchase that book consider using M. Turk on Amazon to pay for it. Do some writing, fill out surveys, and you may get that book for free!

A dollar ...
A dollar saved today @ 32% interest for 30 years will be $4,142.72.

$2 dollars = $8,284
$10 dollars = $41,427
$20 dollars = $82,854
$40 dollars = $165,708
$100 dollars = $414,272

Live within your means. Not everyone shares your dream. People will try to discourage you. You may look like you are falling behind your peers. But don't overspend to support a lifestyle of a successful businessperson…it's expensive.

Silence is Golden

When getting a great deal, sometimes it's best to keep this a secret. Others will try to use this to get their own discount … sometimes you will lose yours.

Banks

Monitor the activity of your business checking account at least a few times a week. All banks are generally the same. They're in business to make money. They will get it with service charges and fees. Your job is to stay on top of this.

In my opinion it's not a good idea to say "don't worry you can pay whenever you can."I'd rather have the money in hand than waking up in the morning wondering who owes me money.

Time Management

There is an industry on time management and you'll most likely come up with many ideas of your own. Some ideas that helped me:

Franklin Covey Planning System

Using a Courier Service

Keep improving your time management techniques and life will get easier. You'll learn this lesson when you are losing sleep after you spent hours talking to your long-winded neighbor.

The Long Road...

Remember that your classmates, family, peers, will be buying homes, cars, starting families as you are sacrificing. They may not be sensitive, as this is a long road to follow. A healthy way to share in each other's success is to define what success is in your own life. It's important to know your definition of success. You are sacrificing today, for benefits for tomorrow. Don't compare yourself to others and don't be so sensitive what others may say about you. Celebrate the freedom of working for yourself, and celebrate the legacy you are creating.

A good read is *The Millionaire Next Door* by Stanley and Danko.

Does it really take five years to break even? Yes, it takes five years to make a profit. Some businesses take even longer. It takes time to set up a business, and something is always coming up.

Don't spend all your money on creating marketing attention. If you won't be able to pay your bills don't gamble.

"He holds victory in store for the upright; he is a shield to those whose walk is blameless, for he guards the course of the just and protects the way of his faithful ones" (Proverbs 2:7-8).

Journal Entry: "Recently we have added 3 new clients and another one is trying us out. The days are busy as the marketing efforts of last year are starting to pay off."

Year One–"Excitement"

"You always quit what you start," my pops said. All my life I've been told that I was a quitter. In my mind, I always felt it was changing to something better. This included changing from baseball (when I didn't make the high school team) to learning the guitar or when I saw I was not going to be the best guitarist I changed to a dental technician. Eventually I changed from dental tech to a pre-dental major. I didn't get in dental school so changed to MBA. Now I was changing from a dental technician to a dental lab owner.

A lot went on in this first year. We assembled a team to do this business. It was an exciting time to pursue something new. I quit my job to run the business full- time. Lessons learned:

Do as much work as possible BEFORE getting an office.

- Honesty is number one
- Pays to be a specialist
- A few trusted advisors help

Year Two– "This is difficult"

"Jack the VC," or venture capitalist, is what they called him. Jack's new black Lexus glistened in the sun as he sped on the California freeway. He bought two cars as a present to himself for completing his MBA, finding a job with a finance company, and getting an 80% raise from his former banking job. He had 20 miles more to go in the 30-mile trip. He would go to their office on Saturdays to help with marketing and to give moral support. He wasn't sure when to get out of this investment...just that he wanted to make a profit. There were concerns. However, he put it out of his mind as he wondered how he would pay for the two cars he had bought, the dream house he was making and the new child he had on the way.

What he knew was he had to find a way to buy a McDonald's franchise.

The dreaded second year. The year business gets boring. The initial excitement of having a business wears off and the hard work begins. My partner, Jack had experienced many life changes since we started the business. The most recent was the death of his mother.

"Do not be yoked together with unbelievers"
(2 Corinthians 6:17).

You are limited to the spiritual, financial, and human capital that is in your business. Are you called to serve in this business? My partner wanted the business to be blessed by a Buddhist monk (his grandma got sick and they had to cancel the trip). Two years later, there is a crack in the wall that starts from the ceiling and drifts down, separating our framed degrees.

Lessons learned:

- You have to do SALES
- Focus on the present business today
- Don't rush the people decisions
- Take your time to make good decisions
- Sometimes you get paid late
- You need to raise prices to improve the quality of your life
- Grow slowly

Year Three– "feels like walking in quicksand"

I'm starting to understand the present situation better. This is a dental lab and should be run as one. We made the lab, so we need more lab work…except the more work we do the more money we lose. The car breaks, equipment breaks, supplies run out, taxes are due, identity theft nearly wiped out our checking account, people calling to go to baseball and basketball games.

After three years, we're still not making a profit. Five years to break even seems like it may be true.

Year Four–still trying

The business is busy in January and is running like a dental lab. We tried to merge with another lab, but it turned out to be a mistake. Old car is still breaking every other month. Business gets busy, then gets slow. Still trying to diversify and having trouble with expenses. Haven't figured out that either I'm not charging enough or we need to get someone who can do the work where we can charge more. This is becoming a boring business that is not making much profit.

I thought, "That's them, that's not me, I'm different."I thought I was smarter and more experienced, was my reaction when told by my professor that it usually takes five years to break even.

Turns out I wasn't.

Year Five–Break even?

Added another room to the office that increased the rent (this will prove to be a mistake). Why did I do it? The landlord recommended it. So, I "planned" to increase marketing, but no time. I moved the lab back home, and then started painting the house. I should have used the time to get the marketing department up and running. We need more clients to cover the additional rent. Finally decided to raise prices! Then all the clients left.

Doing handyman work, researching an import/export business, a tongue cleaner to sell from Italy. Car is still breaking every other month, donating 10% to charity, lab getting slow, day-trading stocks again; costs are going up with the new room. Beware of the project that never ends: fixing up an old house.

It took five long years to break even and now taking on a major painting project! It's good to know if you are attention deficit or have a short attention span. Know thyself to manage thyself.

Year Six–Warren Buffett

Studying the life of Warren Buffett, still looking for an answer for the business, painting continues on the interior of the house. I'm gardening, restoring a bathroom, and dealing with car problems every other month. The revenue is up; we are working for two dentist clients, and the business is still operating from home.

The business is less complicated. There's even profit at the end of the year. The business finally broke above break-even. How? By reducing the rent and car expenses.

Read the entire Bible in one year. Is this a coincidence that the business is doing better?

Year Seven–Warren Buffett, continued

Wish I had made a study of Warren Buffett before starting the business. His lessons on frugality, buying things that go up in value, buying great companies on sale can be a great help to the budding entrepreneur.

This year finally sold car for $125. It was breaking every month or so. Started using a courier service for deliveries. Learning to focus more and the lab is running like a lab.

I'm observing the Sabbath. No work on Sundays after working on Christmas and a crucial piece of equipment broke. No longer working on a day where I'm supposed to honor God.

Discovered the books *Good to Great* and *Built to Last* by Jim Collins. These books should be required reading for anyone with a business.

Year Eight–Frugal

"Have no fear of sudden disaster or of the ruin that over takes the wicked, for the Lord will be your confidence and will keep your foot from being snared" (Proverbs 3:25).

Journal entry from June 12, 2008.

"It's been eight years of starting and running a dental lab. My 25 years of experience, and business education didn't prepare me for this. This is hard work and not easy. I'm trying to save money instead of making more."

Year Nine–Challenging/Difficult

Was a challenging year. No, I would say it was a difficult year. Not so much for the business but for personal reasons. My father, who I had not seen for 25 years or so, died.

Don't let a business ruin your life. I've been so busy that I haven't kept up on my relationships.

Business-wise everything is looking better. I'm starting to pre-save for purchases.

It may be hard to run the business when you are going through emotional times. Give yourself the time to work through it.

In my opinion, you must have a "soul" for your business. It's hard to get through the day-to-day, but attacks on your business will come as a surprise. Every business has competition, and you may be surprised about the forms they take.

The moral to the story is business is not easy. That's why people keep saying, "It's not easy."It's not, even if you know what you are doing.

How do you know when it's time to quit?

When you feel like giving up? Take some time off to reflect.

Year Ten–Closing

Doing mostly lab work and investing in stocks. Saturday, August 14, 2010 closed the lab to manage the assets of the company. The business isn't closing, it's changing. The dental lab suffers from poor economics. For me there are more profits in investing than in running a lab.

Business is not as easy as it looks.

Why?

It's more complicated than it looks. It helps to have prior experience in starting a business. A multitude of people and events go into starting a successful business.

Also, it's hard to plan for the unexpected; you can't predict when a sale will come through the door.

Business is a lot like golf

There may be days when you feel like you are walking in place, not progressing, but are working hard. On these occasional days, I would read and take walks. Don't read anything related to purchasing and investing. Stay away from the sand traps. Then, slowly progress in 3-7 areas. Many times planning and working slowly would get me back to work.

1. Avoid any investment decisions.
2. Slowly progress in 3-7 areas.
3. Don't spend money.

What should you do if a competitor asks for help?

It may lead to consulting services (which has lower costs to set up than a manufacturing business), networking, money, learning, clients and customers, and you may make a friend. Plus, you may serve a different market than your perceived competitor.

Classmates

The wrong person can wreck your business. A wrong person can become a one-person wrecking crew. Countless meetings and wasted energy were spent on a person who was a friend. Be able to do all the jobs or you'll be vulnerable. Working with the wrong people drains time, energy and money.

Competition

It's best to give this area some respect since it can cause many problems. Not all of your classmates, friends and relatives will help you to surpass them. Do you have rivalries or competition that will slow your journey?

Copy your competition.

Going to their stores, reading their advertising and visiting websites are some ways of getting ideas. It's easier to copy than to innovate. If you are the innovator, it takes time, but if you copy, there are multiple sources to get inspiration.

Cross-Trained

It's best to learn everything **BEFORE** starting your business. Then, you can do the most specialized job. If not, you may hear "I don't respect you," "We want a raise, or we will go on strike," or "I'm better than you." This will get under your skin. It did for me. Do yourself a favor and learn the hard stuff before starting your business. It will make life easier.

The activity surrounding your business makes it difficult to learn new things. But you have to invest time, energy and money to keep yourself evolving and growing.

Working as the labor in your business may feel beneath you, but you should be able to do everything. Being dependent on employees will give them a power over you. It's hard, but no one said it would be easy. If you are passionate about your business then learn everything about it.

Data Science Your Invoices & Communications

Data science allows you to research and mine your data. It's the gold, the true informational data that you can use to predict things like slow months, customer vacations as well as industry and sales trends. Treat data like gold and it will reward you. Your data can get you a few extra days of rest of vacation per year.

Entrepreneur Support?

How should you manage a successful career? Develop a support system. An experienced advisor that you can talk to will help. Where can you find one?

- Word of mouth
- Network meetings
- Coaches
- SBA (small business association)

Entrepreneurs

Most don't learn this in school. They have learned it along the way. Their experience has taught them lessons in life and business. Failure has taught them lessons in risk. We must keep learning and improving our skills in order to keep evolving into a successful entrepreneur.

Failure

Make small mistakes

And learn how to fail without losing too much money. Test new concepts for the business. Consider outsourcing the manufacturing while you are testing the demand for a new product. Everyone will make mistakes. Learn to embrace failure and learn from them as a group.

You can recycle mixed paper, electronics, metals, plastics and cardboard for money. You might want to open a savings account for extra money making-opportunities. Then open an account with a discount broker and purchase quality growth companies on sale. Remember that you are in the business of making money.

You will learn the most from your failures. Give yourself permission to fail and try new things. Try to manage small mistakes. Perform tests to minimize risks. Avoid the major mistake that can put you out of business. Most of all, read, talk and learn from the experience of others. Unfortunately, the mistakes you make will be the ones you will remember the most.

Learn from the failure of others.

One of the biggest mistakes I made was to go TOO BIG/TOO EXPENSIVE at the beginning. We purchased a digital shade computer with innovative technology, and we were the first on the West Coast to use it. The computer worked great as a marketing tool. The result was steady revenue. The issue was that the price of the computer was high. We raised $10,000 in capital for the business; the computer cost was $10,000 and was leased with the option to buy. We didn't have any sales for 7 months and had to pay our rent. I still had car insurance, student loans and credit cards; personal expenses can become a drain on the company's assets. In time, the computer broke.

You will learn the most from your mistakes

Focus

Focus, focus, focus. In the real world, *you must focus, but be flexible to finding money-making opportunities for your company (don't close yourself to unexpected opportunities and contacts).* Be open to trying new things, like developing new sales streams.

If you have trouble focusing, try managing your big projects in small pieces. You might want to take your business year by year instead of looking at it as a 10-year plan.

But trying to run many businesses at one time can prove fatal. Making one business succeed is hard; trying to start several magnifies the challenges and headaches. Expenses will start to mount. It's better to focus your resources on one business at a time, but have another one ready in case Plan A doesn't pan out, or you will be out of business.

Focus first, then diversify.

Starting a business is a story of contradictions: focused, yet flexible. It is easier to start without partners, but you need a team to really grow.

Allow yourself plenty of room (and money) to make mistakes in the beginning. You're like a baby learning to walk. There will be many falls and stumbles along the way.

Focused, Yet Flexible

In your business journey you may hear that you have to be focused. Other times, you may hear that you have to be flexible. I often wondered how you can be both focused and flexible at the same time. It's important to be focused on keeping your marketing going, continuous learning, the day-to-day grind of daily business, but be flexible in opportunities that come your way.

Frugal

Don't expand before sales. It's common to think that you will get more space and then increase your marketing efforts. This is a trap. Make do with less; be frugal. It is much easier to save a dollar than to earn one.

Gratitude

"How am I to be happy when my business is still not making a profit? There's so much to do, but I know that I should be gracious and thankful." For me, it was hard to be happy in the moment. A lot of unnecessary time and energy was spent on "people" problems.

It is important to know how to show appreciation to the people God has placed in your life; they are there for a reason. They have sacrificed and helped you to get to this point. No one will work at your company forever. Show appreciation to people while they are there. At this point, you may be breaking even or even making profits and learning how your business works. During the slow times, you can relax, listen and learn.

Your Landlord

A landlord can be an ally or an enemy. Do what you can to start on the right foot and avoid unnecessary conflict. There are times when you will be working with each other. It helps to have a working relationship with their staff. Keys, upgrades to your office, paint, nameplates, your name in a directory and letting people in if they are locked out are things you need from them. Don't forget to negotiate. A good landlord can make it a joy to go to the office; some may even make your coffee. A bad landlord will be raising the rent again.

Legacy, Leader, or Laggard?

The dental lab field was once dominated by trade people opening their own businesses. In a strategic finance class, our instructor said, "If "robotics and outsourcing enter the field, it's time to flee." Add consolidation, and that's the lab field. Before, dental technicians made crowns by hand. Now, computers make them with instructions from scanners. It's a changing industry.

If I had to do it over, I would:

1. Set up a consulting and marketing service company while working at my present job.
2. Conduct a test marketing campaign while working.
3. Find out what clients are looking for and what their major problems are.
4. Become an expert on the product.
5. Open a product-related business.
6. Get an office.

Once there were enough clients to pay for rent, I would get an office. The office space would be small. We would outsource labor. I would try to get by with less.

"If you see robotics and outsourcing entering your industry, flee the industry."

Was it true? Yes, computers are taking the place of dental technicians. There's an increasing trend of work being sent overseas. Competing with overseas competition makes it difficult to raise prices.

Legal

Get a good lawyer and be open to opportunities. Talk with your board of advisors. Your decision-making skills will evolve and improve over time.

Having a good lawyer will save you time and worry. Consider joining a legal network if the costs are too high. Later, you can improve your legal representation if your business gets more complex.

Where do I get a license?

To open a business account at a bank, you first have to check if the business name is available. Go to the board of equalization, pay the fee, and then publish in a local newspaper. The next step is to register your business at your local city hall. Now you're ready to open a checking account. Be sure to request an experienced person to open your account. Get the manager or an experienced banker, and you should be up and running in a few weeks with your checks. It helps to confirm that everything is going as expected and if they need additional information.

Start slowly and make adjustments as your company evolves and develops.

Timeline:

1. License with Board of Equalization
2. License from City Hall
3. Open a business bank account.
4. Marketing materials
5. Start marketing your business.
6. Sales
7. Office

Life Plan

Consider making a life plan. Try to align both a business and a life plan for a happy and rewarding life. Decide what kind of life you want to live and the business you are trying to create. Don't leave it to chance.

Put those music dreams on hold.

During the first years 2-5 years of your business when the day-to-day boredom of business is draining your ambition, motivation and sanity, former dreams of becoming a musician may come back. I have seen several entrepreneurs who think that they will create the next break-out CD only to find that they wasted company time and money. Upon reflection, they regret the time and money it took to produce the CD. It's sad to see. They could have started new businesses, financed new departments, found more customers and clients, invested money in stocks and put aside money for the next tax payment. After you have produced your music, you most likely will have to market this just like your original business.

A music project will probably not produce a nice return on an investment. Do a side-by-side comparison between buying the stocks of a growth company bought on sale compared to a music project. Put your musical goals on hold for a time when you can devote your full attention. The music business is filled with competitors, and rarely will someone come out ahead who is doing it part-time.

Remember that one day before the rent is due, you may be going door to door trying to sell your product. Wouldn't it have been a better decision to buy those shares of Google at a cheap price then waiting for the price to go up and reinvesting the profits in the business?

A creative business is a challenge to manage. And a technical business requires a lot of reading and expertise to keep up with developments and competition. A creative and technical business is a bad combination. A business that's hard to manage, requires a large investment and makes it difficult to raise prices. If I were to do it again, I would find a business that is:

- Fun and passionately interesting
- Not creative
- Not technical
- You can raise prices with inflation
- You have a competitive advantage
- Good profits

Manage thyself.
Manage your emotions, motivation and mood to maintain a positive outlook. I've noticed that the full moon makes me moody sometimes.

You will be overworked, under-appreciated and will lead people who enjoy their weekends while you are working. There may be a time when you sacrifice so your workers can have money to live the life they want. You are working so you can pay them.

Manage your time.
Your clients/customers eventually take up a majority of your time. This leaves some time for self-improvement, family, friends, time to develop the company, marketing, etc.

Develop yourself and the company and keep growing. Develop a personal improvement schedule. Look into getting a personal coach if necessary.

Money talks.
It buys the best people. In the beginning, you should do everything then train and delegate.

Have fun! Celebrate your freedom, the opportunity to put your skills to use and cutting your own path.

Organization

How many hats are you wearing?
Make your company's organizational chart. You will be surprised at how many hats you are wearing. Strive to wear fewer hats and make your company stronger. Do what you do best and let go. Build the team. In cases where it is difficult to find talent, consider paying a company to help you find more time and energy. You can increase your working hours this way. Everyone has the same amount of hours, and, in time, you will use all of yours. In a great team, everyone's efforts are multiplied.

Find something you are deeply passionate about.
Then figure out a way to make a living around it. If I started as a service business providing marketing support then branched into a product business, it would have been cheaper. The outcome would be a wider network, more support and more training opportunity within the dental field.

People

Don't take on VCs as partners. In the start-up phase, you will need people to help you move a mountain not watch you moving it by yourself. You need people who will work with you. A spouse is the ideal partner, as they have your best interests at heart.

People are hard to lead.

They will find something that they are better at in order to disrespect you. So be prepared to do most of the work. Save yourself the stress and money. Put off hiring sales staff as long as possible. No one sells your personal brand and company like you. People prefer to work with the founder of the company.

What should you do if someone isn't working out?

Check yourself. Are you really offering a great example of leadership to them? Try watching Ken Blanchard on YouTube. There is a wealth of knowledge on YouTube from Ken Blanchard on leadership from Harvard Business School on leading to entrepreneur panels from Stanford Business School.

When it doesn't work out...

"My dear brothers, take note of this: Everyone should be quick to listen, slow to speak and slow to become angry, for anger does not bring about the righteous life that God desires" (James 1:19-20).

Picking wrong people will drain your energy. Be open-minded when you have made a mistake. How can you keep this bridge open and give dignity to the person involved? Sometimes this is a relative or a friend. You must get trustworthy, disciplined, honest and hard working people on board.

Phone Calls

Always be prepared to answer a sales-related question. Don't be on the golf course when a client is calling while busy at work. This gives an impression that you have made it and are not hungry. It never pays to drink alcohol while at work. Invariably, that client you are waiting for will call when you had one too many.

Have a policy how to handle those sales-related calls. In time, there will be many of them, and they call at the busiest moments.

Don't price yourself on the low end.

When determining your price, make sure that you are making a profit. After expenses, now decide how much profit you want to make. This is how your life improves. And don't forget to raise prices a little every year.

If you are losing money on each sale, keep your sales low until you get the skills and confidence to raise your prices. Being busy while not making money is not rewarding, and it's risky.

What's your price of having a good quality of life? Is it $80 or $180 a month? How about $8,000? At what point can the entrepreneur start to delegate, hire a sales assistant, focus on marketing or even delegate marketing?

When you raise prices, be prepared for your customers to be unhappy. How do you feel when someone raises prices on you? That's right- it's like they are stealing your lunch.

The lowest price can mean the lowest quality of life unless you are making a profit and you sell a lot.

Think that you are the best! You bring value to those around you, and doing business with you will pay off in the end. Be sure that you are improving your product, raising prices regularly and growing as a person and a business owner.

Don't be afraid to charge what you are worth, but know why your clients are sending you work. You may price yourself out of a sale. Communicate with your customers/clients in these instances.

Commit to leading your best life. Don't be afraid to raise prices from time to time (the best way is to raise a little on a consistent basis). This is keeping up with living expenses. You need money for your family and your employees. No profits means no raises, and your employees will ask for more money.

Reading People

It's important to know how to read people. You must be flexible and willing to compromise. Sometimes, you have to assume some debt to pay investors in order to keep relationships stable.

Reading people is not easy when you are busy, but it can be a problem later. Paying someone off who isn't working out is better than an unexpected crisis. Not all people and situations will work out. It's best to move on and be on your way.

Sacrifice

Are you prepared to give up a regular paycheck for a life of uncertainty and risk? You sometimes will do the low-level work so your workers can continue to be employed. Then, they don't respect you.

You may not be able to sleep for a night
When you are swamped with business. It can happen.

It helps if you have people to call for support. Visualize a worst case scenario and have a plan in place.

- Courier
- Shipping options
- Food
- Labor
- Phones
- Childcare
- Household help

Think McDonalds at lunch rush.

What if you can't do all the work?

Make **sleep** work for you. Develop a routine. Experiment in order to get the maximum rest from sleep. Wake up refreshed and start early. Organize the night before.

Socializing

You may not feel up to it when a classmate or relative invites you to celebrate their new house, wedding or kids, during a time when you are not sure if your business is going to make it. What's shocking is that in a social setting, you'll be asked what you do for a living? Most likely, you will reply, "I…own my own business." "Oh, what kind of business?" "It's a dog grooming (fill in the blank) business." Don't be surprised about the strange looks you may get. Keep the conversation going, and it may get worse when you are trying to describe the company that you visualized at the outset. The business may have changed dramatically.

Be wary of your classmate who wants to golf or attend sports events, on your free time. How many products and services do you have to sell to pay for the outing? Let's say that you are planning to go to a baseball game with your classmate.

Your ticket costs $25, plus $15 for food and $10 for parking for a total of $50 each. If you produce hats at $50 each and make a profit of $10 per unit, you will have to manufacture five hats just to pay for your outing.

Stress

As an employee, I never had a sinus headache. As an entrepreneur, I started getting them. You can't predict your next sale or when you will be paid. This uncertainty and other stressors can lead to sinus headaches. Sinus headaches are debilitating and make it difficult to carry on regular business activities. Your eyes, ears and teeth hurt and are accompanied with a throbbing headache. Good medications help to relieve the pain. You will sometimes have to work when sick.

It helps to talk to people who can help you. On those days where you may be sick it's always a good idea to have people you can call for backup. These can include trusted advisors, senior friends or, better, yet a company you can call.

More business can mean more headaches.
More clients mean more demands on your time, emotions, energy and money (it takes money to finance more work). The demands on your time will be multiplied. You will have more responsibilities. If you are losing money on each sale, doing more work may result in a bigger loss. A large order is riskier and requires more capital. Plus, what if the customer fails to pay?

Survey and ask your customers for input. Ask questions, as you are in a working "partnership." How can you make a better shopping/buying experience? What would make their day?

Technology

Automate everything. These simple tasks like mail, bills and email can take up a lot of time.

Amazon, Bank Account, Craigslist and EBay
To keep up with these accounts as well as your technology needs takes time. Add your Facebook account, email and news and you will see how it pays to be disciplined. Your goal should be to manage these demands on your time.

Time is money.

Schedule a time every week when you will to do your marketing. A better idea is to do some everyday, but it's difficult when you are busy. This should be separate from sales-related activities.

It's easier to do your marketing everyday as a group, but it's not always possible. It's crucial to the survival of your business to keep up your marketing efforts, or you may find yourself without any clients. You may want to consider hiring a part-time student or a senior or delegate to a member of your team.

Be careful how you spend your time.

A time audit will show what you are doing during the day. My time was not used wisely when I spent time with people that did not help in my business. How do you know if someone is draining your time? Spending time on something or someone isn't helpful if it isn't helping your business grow, making contacts for the future, having fun or making money.

Vacations

Give yourself a break; take at least one vacation a year. It's easy to keep working year after year. Raise prices, take a break, be refreshed and ready to go.

"A little sleep, a little slumber, a little folding of the hands to rest-and poverty will come on you like a bandit and scarcity like an armed man" (Proverbs 24:33-34).

Restate:

- **Focus**, *focus*, **Focus** once you decide on your current business.

- Be flexible about finding your niche.

- Business plans aren't a guarantee for success: Don't rely on them.

- Assemble a great team.

- Honesty always! If you are not honest with clients and mentors, you will not be able to ask for help.

- Walk before you run-start small and grow little by little.

- Fail fast.

- Manage your marketing.

- Don't run out of money.

- It's not easy...don't let it drive you out of your mind.

- Find people you can trust.

- Sometimes, thinking too BIG can make you unhappy. Grow slowly and be more content. Big projects can mean BIG MISTAKES. Less is sometimes more and safer.

FINAL THOUGHTS

What I learned during the time of business:

1. Undercapitalized in finances means no money to grow and develop the business.
2. Undercapitalized in Human Resources means no people to grow your company.
3. Business gets boring in year two.
4. A great team wins…but is hard to assemble.
5. It's better to hire a company than to rely on people.
6. Make time for yourself. Weekends are a time to catch up on work, planning, resting, spending time with family and friends, pursuing hobbies and interests.
7. Self-esteem and prices go hand in hand. Therefore manage your self-esteem.
8. Don't let your clients lower your self-esteem to get lower prices.
9. Dream…have long-term and short-term goals for yourself and your family.
10. When your peers are buying homes, starting families…you may be cash poor.
11. Travel can help to recharge the soul.

12. It takes about six months for marketing to produce results.
13. Your character is important.
14. Entrepreneurship is a lonely business. Make friends who are part of the business.
15. You really have to focus.
16. Occasionally it helps to give back and help people.

It helps to have a customer-first mentality. It helps to love people.

Closing thoughts...

I hope readers will either be encouraged to plan for their future business or will be discouraged and will therefore stay with their present job.

So what happened to the team I put together after 10 years? My VC partner stopped showing up after the second year. Our silent partner was silent; my MBA classmate moved to Taiwan. The dental technician quit, and my previous employer passed away. At the end of year 10 I was busy working on my own, producing ceramic crowns for two dentists.

I had closed the lab, sold its contents, and taken a few years off to invest in stocks full-time. The book project is to help folks on their journey to a faith-based business. If not managed properly, it can be a life of struggles. Done right, and the possibilities are endless.

My prayer for you, the reader, is that you will find your success. It may be financial, like setting up a foundation to bless others, raising a family, or having the freedom of becoming your own boss. Please don't forget your mental and spiritual health as you seek God's will and leading in your life. May God be with you in all you do!

Books I found Helpful

The Bible

All Warren Buffett books

Good to Great & Built to Last by Jim Collins

Benjamin Franklin books

The 7 Habits of Highly Effective People by Stephen Covey

How to Stop Worrying and Start Living and *How to Make Friends and Influence People* by Dale Carnegie

The Millionaire Next Door by Stanley and Danko

Avoiding Mistakes in Your Small Business by David Carlson

Rules of Thumb by Alan Webber

Big Book on Small Business by Tom Gegax

4 Essential Traits of Entrepreneurial Thinking by Cliff Michaels

E-Myth by Michael Gerber

Videos- YouTube

Ken Blanchard on Leadership

Stanford Entrepreneur Panels

Harvard Business School Leadership

Grant Cardone and Zig Ziglar on Sales

Richard Branson entrepreneur

TED videos

Entrepreneur Emotional Roller Coaster

Websites

StartYourOwnBusiness.org

GrowYourOwnBusiness.org

Jim Collins.com

Biography

I had experience in my industry (over 20 years), went to dental lab school, applied to dental school, and wasn't accepted. So, I changed my major and earned MBA/BS/AA degrees in business. Everything in my education, experience, and training was in the dental lab industry. What I lacked was experience in *starting a business.* The book knowledge was different from the application knowledge that was required to start a successful business. I was unaware and will share with you what worked and what didn't. I share my experience in hopes that you will learn from my mistakes and will be prepared for the challenges that await you. If you have any ideas on how I can make this book better or want to share anything about the book please contact me. I can be reached at:

www.thebirthofabusiness.blogspot.com

APPENDIX

100 Tips for your Business:

1. Your friend may let you down plan for it.
2. Help often comes from unexpected sources.
3. Never depend on one person.
4. Surround yourself with loyal people.
5. Prepare for January it's the most expensive month.
6. Don't get an office until you absolutely need one.
7. Don't overspend on marketing.
8. Have a back up plan.
9. You will be very busy try Franklin Covey planners.
10. You will be stressed
11. You may develop headaches.
12. Listen to your people.
13. Tough times make you stronger.
14. Failing often leads to success.
15. Buy things that will go up in value.
16. Sell inventory while it has value.
17. How much profit are you making per sale?
18. Do your due diligence in profits and losses.
19. Be an open book financially.
20. Let everyone be involved in financial matters.
21. Receive wise council.

22. Beware of the hidden agenda.
23. Business can be brutal get a good lawyer.
24. Human hours collect these to increase your wealth.
25. Don't play golf until you can pay with your personal funds.
26. Work smarter and longer.
27. Find ways to be more productive.
28. Learn to stretch a dollar.
29. Wait at least a week before buying it.
30. Can you work with your competitors?
31. Are you better than the competition?
32. Streamline your mail.
33. Celebrate accomplishments.
34. Partner with your clients.
35. Create value for your clients.
36. Keep junk mail for scrap paper.
37. Avoid the crowds; shop and do your errands when stores are slow.
38. Walk if you can.
39. Don't ever run out of money. Keep your credit cards with a low balance for emergencies.
40. Beware of the big order it can be risky.
41. Pre-save for large purchases and buy on sale.
42. Darwin's survival of the fittest. Adapt to survive.
43. Partner's wives are your partners.
44. Become a Marketing and Sales machine.
45. Develop a routine.
46. Always be reading.
47. Always be learning.
48. Live an interesting life.
49. Be an interesting person.
50. Prepare for the next project.
51. Develop your leadership skills.

52. Know who you can trust.
53. Know who your real friends are.
54. Learn to read people.
55. Do the hard thing and specialize.
56. Surround yourself with positive people.
57. Enjoy your slow times, but work hard on sales.
58. Don't stress over things you can't control.
59. Part-time job.
60. Emergency account.
61. Saving accounts.
62. Business is about competition.
63. Know what your exit plan is.
64. Write your business plan in pencil in case it changes.
65. Learn to accept change.
66. Have regular dental check ups.
67. Get your medical exams if over 50.
68. Do one thing well.
69. Be the best at what you are doing now.
70. A common problem: sales too low.
71. A common solution: increase marketing.
72. If you have passion, then work is fun.
73. Never lie.
74. Charge for your work.
75. Write and give gifts
76. Have a plan B ready, just in case.
77. What would it take for you to be the best?
78. Use ROI to compare investments.
79. Use time to think about purchases.
80. Technology: start small and grow.
81. Read outside of your industry.
82. Love your people.
83. Show and tell appreciation.
84. Melatonin to help with sleeping.

85. Overlap projects.
86. Embrace a frugal mentality.
87. Everything sells!
88. Ask for referrals.
89. Sales.
90. Patience.
91. Take time out for innovation thinking time.
92. Enjoy your free time.
93. Take the day off.
94. Develop your marketing brand.
95. Spend time with those in your business.
96. Thank those who are helping you.
97. Be an expert.
98. Learn to work fast.
99. Learn how to accept help.
100.   Update your business plan yearly.

SELF-CONTRACT

I (name) _____have the PASSION in (industry) _____ to FOCUS on a _____ business.

I enjoy_____ more than anything right now. I will dedicate my best effort and will sacrifice at least 1 year, after which I can either run for 2 years or sell it. I UNDERSTAND that it can take up to 5 years to break-even. We will review contracts at 2 years; 5 years and 10 years.

I understand that if I enjoy my work, have a passion for it, and have special abilities it will be easier to focus my time and effort on it. It will take a lot of time, energy, money and sacrifice.

I agree to focus and commit on _____business for_____ years of months.

X_____ Date:

May God Bless You in Your Business!

STACKING THE ODDS IN YOUR FAVOR

About 50% of small businesses will make it to 5 years. This is about the time it takes to break-even and make a small profit. After the 5th year, your odds of survival and success will improve even more!

How to improve your odds?

1. Find a trusted_____ who you can regularly ask for advice.
2. Have a trustworthy _____ of employees (3-4) that can help your business.
3. Have trustworthy _____ that will invest time, money, and will sacrifice with you for the long term (over 10 years).
4. Have a partner that complements your skills and _____.
5. Have enough _____ to be able to survive 6 months or more.
6. _____ credit card debts.
7. Frugal _____.
8. _____ in God.
9. Have a _____ team that will work with you in keeping your marketing department active and growing.
10. Have _____ starting and managing a business.
11. Have a deep _____for your business.
12. Adopt a _____ of learning.

Answers

1.	Advisor	5.	Capital	9.	Marketing
2.	Group	6.	No	10.	Experience
3.	Partners	7.	Living	11.	Passion
4.	Weaknesses	8.	Faith	12.	Lifetime

CHECK UP

If you have bad results or questions you may want to discuss them with your team of specialists: CPA; Consultant; Marketing agency; Mentor; Advisors; Pastor; Therapists, board, team. Go get help before it gets out of control.

1. I'm working longer hours: Y/N
2. I have more money to invest every month: Y/N
3. I often find myself stressed: Y/N
4. I often bounce checks: Y/N
5. Have you talked to your customers: Y/N
6. Are you doing sales everyday: Y/N
7. Growing as a leader: Y/N
8. Reading any new books: Y/N
9. Meeting with advisors: Y/N
10. Keeping up with partners & investors: Y/N
11. Improving your team: Y/N
12. Getting more tired: Y/N
13. Raised prices this year: Y/N
14. Able to pay your salary: Y/N
15. Delegating more: Y/N
16. Making new relationships: Y/N
17. Getting away from the business: Y/N
18. Able to remember people's names: Y/N
19. Exercising regularly: Y/N
20. Improving the quality of business: Y/N
21. Can the business function without you: Y/N
22. Are you at your ideal weight: Y/N
23. Time alone to reflect once a week: Y/N
24. Selling or auctioning inventory: Y/N
25. Know your exit plan: Y/N

Hold your mistakes close and dear to you. Your mistakes are your teachers. Make adjustments to your business. They will guide you as you progress along your journey.

CHECKLIST

- ☐ You are Focused
- ☐ Flexible in how you will make money (at least at the beginning)
- ☐ You have made a Business Plan
- ☐ Can you put aside your Business Plan?
- ☐ Have you started a business before?
- ☐ Do you have access to an advisor?
- ☐ Do you know what your customer's biggest problem is?
- ☐ Do you have an answer to their problem?
- ☐ Do you have regular clients/customers?
- ☐ Avoidance to credit card debt
- ☐ Are you frugal? Can you can stretch a dollar?
- ☐ You are prepared to be a Salesperson
- ☐ Pick partners that complement your skills
- ☐ Pick partners like you would a friend: getting along is more fun!
- ☐ Pick your partners like you would a spouse
- ☐ Pick a partner that will work as hard as you
- ☐ Have a legal contract on your working relationship.
- ☐ Do you have a Plan B if your partner(s) leave?
- ☐ Know who you can trust
- ☐ Your business is not meant to be kept on a life support system
- ☐ Parents are sometimes not ideal partners
- ☐ Parents have trouble being led by their children
- ☐ Classmates are really your competition/peers.
- ☐ Are you an expert in your product?
- ☐ Do your learning before you open for business

RESEARCH

What Makes for a Good Business?
Your business is a:
Assign a point total: A=5 points; F=1 point

Lends itself to marketing:
Easy to train people:
Low overhead (don't want to spend on equipment):
Good growth opportunities:
Not creative or technical:
Not technology driven:
Growth industry:
Ability and interest to focus long term?
Can you focus on this one thing well?
Capital to invest
Can be repeated several times
Does not need a physical location
ROI of 20% or better
Interesting and challenging
Increase price with inflation
Ability to serve others
Ease of attracting people
Doesn't require a lot of licenses
Matches experience
Can hire experience
Lends to charity work
Intellectually stimulating

Total score
Highest score

Compare with results from public company shares and other businesses.

QUIZ

1. What are the important things that should be done BEFORE finding a location?
   A. Business Plan
   B. Sales
   C. Money
   D. People
   E. All

2. What is crucial for Entrepreneurial Success?
   A. Focus
   B. Commitment
   C. A great team
   D. Frugality
   E. All

3. What are important things that lead to Entrepreneurial Success?
   A. Experience in the field
   B. Experience in starting a business
   C. Supportive family and friends
   D. Network
   E. All

4. What can hurt your chances of a successful business?
   A. Inability to focus on the job at hand
   B. Lack of discipline
   C. Excessive use of credit cards
   D. Picking the wrong partners
   E. All

5. What traits are desirable in an Entrepreneur?
A. Honesty
B. Love people
C. Frugal
D. Effective time management
E. All

Answers: All E

Where and what are your potholes, sand traps, places you can die, monsters?
   1. Too much debt
   2. Low sales
   3. Low capital
   4. Low profits
   5. Not enough people on your team
   6. Not enough experience